अस्तित्व के रंग

Colours of Existence

Varruna Prasad

BookLeaf Publishing
India | USA | UK

Made with ❤ on the BookLeaf Publishing Platform
www.bookleafpub.in
www.bookleafpub.com

Dedication

To My Daughter

Preface

"Astitva Ke Rang" is a heartfelt exploration of the many hues that color our existence—joy and sorrow, strength and vulnerability, hope and despair. Each poem in this collection is a reflection, a thought, and a whisper of the soul seeking expression in a complex world.

These verses emerged gradually—sometimes as quiet musings in solitude, sometimes as fierce storms of feeling that demanded voice. Through the pages of this book, I have tried to capture the evolving essence of being—*astitva*—as it shifts, grows, and redefines itself in the face of life's ever-changing circumstances.

"Astitva Ke Rang" is not merely a poetic journey—it is a mirror to the self, and perhaps, if you pause and listen closely, a mirror to your own thoughts and feelings as well.

I hope that as you read these poems, you find not just the poet's voice, but echoes of your own. May these colours of existence leave a lasting impression on your heart.

With gratitude,

Varruna Prasad

Acknowledgements

I offer my deepest gratitude to everyone who stood beside me, not just in writing my book but in life.
To my family, for their patience and love. To my friends, for their belief when I had none.
To the inner voice that kept whispering, *"keep going."*
To every reader who pauses to feel these words—you make this journey meaningful.
And to the moments of stillness, pain, and light that shaped this collection—thank you for finding me.

1. एक और छलांग

रात है काली,
गहरा है अँधेरा,
डर का हर पल पे है पहरा।
रुक जाऊँ, लौट जाऊँ,
अब पीछे क़दम ले जाऊँ?
अब कैसे एक और छलांग लगाऊँ?

आगे बढ़ूँ तो अगर गिर जाऊँ,
शायद टूट जाऊँ, फिर से चोट खाऊँ।
अब न कोई और छलांग लगाऊँ।

रास्ते में हैं पत्थर,
हार भी कर रहा पुकार।
इन रोड़ों को कहाँ हटाऊँ?
नहीं वो ताक़त कि और छलांग लगाऊँ।

डर से काँपती हर नस में,
कहीं एक चिंगारी भी है,
जो चाहे कि मैं अपना सिर उठाऊँ,
आज एक और छलांग लगाऊँ।

कहीं छुपी है हिम्मत,
जो कहे कि मैं लड़ जाऊँ,
शायद जीत जाऊँ,

शायद जी पाऊँ।

चाहे आज मिट जाऊँ,
सिरफिरी कहलाऊँ,
अब लौट के न जाऊँ,
हौसले का तिरंगा लहराऊँ।

आज ठानी मैंने – एक और छलांग लगाऊँ।

(छलांग-Jump, रोड़ों -Stones, चिंगारी-Spark)

2. Ek Aur Chalang

Raat hai Kaali
Gehra hai andhera
Darr ka har pal pe hai pehra
Ruk jau, Laut jau
Ab peeche kadam le jau
Ab kaise ek aur chalang lagau

Aage badhu toh agar gir jau
Shayad tuut jau, phir se chot khau
Ab na koi aur chalang lagau

Raste mein hai pathar
Haar bhi kar raha pukar
In roro ko kaha hatau
Nahi woh takat ki aur chalang lagau

Darr se kapti har nas mein
Kahi ek chingari bhi hai
Jo chahe ki main apna sir utahu
Aaj ek aur chalang lagau

Kahi chupi hai himmat
Jo kahe ki main lad jau
Shayad jeet jau

Shayad jee pau

Chahe aaj mit jau
Sarphiri kehlau
Ab laut ke na jau
Hausle ka tiranga lehrau

Aaj thanli maine, Ek aur chalang lagau

3. हार

फिर एक बार,
मेरे दरवाज़े पे दस्तक दे रही हार
क्यों नहीं चाहता संसार
कि मैं जीतूँ एक बार

क्यों मेरी मेहनत हो जाती बेकार
इस पक्षपात की दुनिया में
धराशाई हूँ बार-बार
ऐसा क्या करूँ कि किस्मत पलटे
मन पूछता है पुकार

फिर एक बार,
मेरे दरवाज़े पे दस्तक दे रही हार
क्यों नहीं चाहता संसार
कि मैं जीतूँ एक बार

जो किस्मत बदले मेरी
ढूँढ रही हूँ एक चमत्कार
डर है कहीं जीत न पाऊँ
क्या करूँ ऐसा कि चूमूँ शिखर एक बार

फिर एक बार,
मेरे दरवाज़े पे दस्तक दे रही हार
सोचती हूँ कहीं कोई कमी रह जाती हर बार

और वही तो दिलाती नहीं मुझे हार

फिर एक बार,
मेरे दरवाज़े पे दस्तक दे रही हार
पर क्या मैं मान लूँ
इस हार को जीवन का सार?

पर अब मैं करती हूँ स्वीकार
कुछ ग़लतियाँ होंगी मेरी
जिन्हें मैं सुधारूँगी इस बार

फिर एक बार,
मेरे दरवाज़े पे दस्तक दे रही हार
पर मैं नहीं मान रही हार

(पक्षपात – Partialily, धराशाई- Collapse)

4. Haar

Phir ek baar,
Mere darwaze pe dastak de rahi haar
Kyu nahi chahta sansaar
Ki main jeetu ek baar

Kyu meri mehnat ho jati bekar
Is pakshpat ki duniya mein
Dharaashaee hu baar baar
Aisa kya karu ki kismat palte
Mann puchta hai pukar

Phir ek baar,
Mere darwaze pe dastak de rahi haar
Kyu nahi chahta sansaar
Ki main jeetu ek baar

Jo kismat badle meri
Dunde rahi hu ek chamatkar
Darr hai kahi jeet na pau
Kya karu aisa ki chumu shikhar ek baar

Phir ek baar,
Mere darwaze pe dastak de rahi haar
Sochati hu kahi koi kamee reh jati har baar

Aur wahi toh dilati nahi mujhe haar

Phir ek baar,
Mere darwaze pe dastak de rahi haar
Pur kya main maan lu
Is haar ko jeevan ka saar?

Par ab main karti hu sweekar
Kuch galtiya hogi meri
Jinhe main sudharungi iss baar

Phir ek baar,
Mere darwaze pe dastak de rahi haar
Pur main nahi maan rahi haar

5. कब तक

कब तक इस दर्द में जियूँ
कब तक इन छालो की टीस सहूँ
बेड़िया बन गई है पैरों की
कब मैं आज़ाद उड़ूँ

खुरेदता रहता है माँ इन बीते घावों को
जलता है दिल गुज़रे वक्त की आहट से
डर है कि ज़िंदगी यूही न बहा जाए
हर हँसी की दुआ, छोटी न पड़ जाए

कब तक इस दर्द में जियूँ
कब तक इन छालो की टीस सहूँ
बेड़िया बन गई है पैरों की
कब मैं आज़ाद उड़ूँ

पर सोचती हूँ तो लगता है
वक्त मलहम तो बन गया है
बिना आहट किए कुछ जलन कम कर गया है

उम्मीद यही कि जाते हर साल में
थोड़ा कम हो जाए ये मलाल
शायद बूढ़ापा आने से पहले
मैं हो जाऊं खुशहाल

शायद अब ज़्यादा दर्द में न जियूँ
अब टीस न सहूँ
पैरों में पंख लग जाएं
आने वाले उस वक्त की राह तकूं मैं

(टीस-Pain, बेड़िया-Chains)

6. Kab Tak

Kab tak is dard mein jiyu
Kab tak in chhalo ki tees sahu
Bediya bann gai hai pairyo ki
Kab main aazad udu

Kuredta rahtha hai maan in beete ghao ko
Jalta hai dil gujre waqt ki aahat se
Darr hai ki zindagi you hi na behjaye
Har hasi ki dua choti na pad jaye

Kab tak is dard mein jiyu
Kab tak in chaloo ki tees sahu
Bediya bann gai hai pairyo ki
Kab main aazad udu

Par sochati hu toh lagta hai
Waqt malham toh ban gaya hai
Bina aahat kiye kuch jalan kam kar gaya hai

Umeed yehi ki jate har saal mein
Thoda kam ho jaye yeah malal
Shayad budhapa aane se pehle
Main ho jau khushaal

Shayad ab zyada dard mein na jiyu
Ab tees na sahu
Pairyo mein pankh lag jaya
Aane wale uss waqt ki rah taku main

7. डूबी उम्मीदें

हर ख्वाब था,जो टूट गया
हर लम्हा मुझसे रूठ गया
उम्मीद की डोर बांधूं तो किस छोर से
अब तो हर किनारा भी डूब गया

किस राह पे चलूं अब
हर तरफ है अंधकार
प्रेरणा किससे लूं, सब कर रहे तिरस्कार

लग रहा है एक ही कश्ती
और छोर नहीं पास
कैसे मैं पार आ जाऊं
किस से लगाऊं आस

हर ख्वाब जो था टूट गया
हर लम्हा मुझसे रूठ गया
उम्मीद की डोर बांधूं तो किस चोर से
अब तो हर किनारा भी डूब गया

हिम्मत भी मेरी हार गई
किस्मत ने जो मेरे साथ न रही
कैसे अब अपनी दुनिया सजाऊं
कहीं इस कश्ती के साथ मैं न डूब जाऊं

करती हूँ गुहार
है कोई जो बचाए मेरा संसार
टूट रही हूँ मैं
बिखर जाऊंगी इस बार

(तिरस्कार-Insult, गुहार -Appeal)

8. Doobi Umeede

Har khab jo tha tuut gaya
Har lamha mujhe se ruth gaya
Umeed ki dor bandhu toh kis chor se
Ab toh har kinara bhi dub gaya

Kiss rah pe chalu ab
Har taraf hai andhkar
Prerna kissse lu, sab kar rahe tiraskaar

Lag raha hai ek hai kasti
Aur chhor nahi pass
Kaise mein paar aa jau
Kiss se lagau aas

Har khab jo tha tuut gaya
Har lamha mujhe se ruth gaya
Umeed ki dor bandhu toh kis chor se
Ab toh har kinara bhi dub gaya

Himmat bhi meri haar gayi
Kismat ne jo mere saath na rahi
Kaise ab apni duniya sajau
Kahi iss kasti ke saath mein na duub jau

Karti hu guhaar
Hai koi jo bachaeya mere sansaar
Tut rahi hu main
Bikhar jaugi iss baar

9. बीता वक़्त

चाहे आपकी बातों में अब न वो बात हो
चाहे आपकी राहों में अब न कोई साथ हो
मुड़ कर देखिए ज़रा
जो दिए आपने रोशन किए,
वो आज भी टिमटिमा रहे हैं

जो मज़मा आपकी चौखट पर था,
भले आज किसी और के पास है
पर वक़्त के पन्नों में, झाँकिए एक बार
आपका नाम अभी भी वहीं लिखा है

नहीं ज़ाया हुई आपकी मेहनत
कई और हैं जो चले हैं आपकी राहों पर
मिल रही है उन्हें हिम्मत
आपने जो झेली मुश्किलें
उनसे सीख दूसरे भी ले रहे

चाहे आपकी बातों में अब न वो बात हो
चाहे आपकी राहों में अब न कोई साथ हो
चाहे आपके नाम से जुड़े वो जज़्बात न हो
आप वहीं हो, जिसने फतह की थी वो मंज़िलें

10. Beeta Waqt

Chahe aapki baato mein ab na woh baat ho
Chahe aapki raho mein ab na koi saath ho
Mud kar dekkhye Zara
Jo diye aap na roshan kiye,
woh aaj bhi tim tima rahe hai
Jo mazma aapki chukhat par tha,
Bhale aaj kisi aur ke pass hai

Par waqt ke pano mein, jhakiye ek baar
Aap ka naam abhi bhi wahi likha hai

Nahi zaya hui aapki mehnat
Kai aur hai jo chale hai aapki raho par
Mil rahi hai unhe himmat

Aap ne jo jheli muskile
Unse seekh dusre bhi le rahi

Chahe aapki baato mein ab na woh baat ho
Chahe aapki raho mein ab na koi saath ho
Chahe aapke naam se jude woh jazbaat nah o
Aap wahi ho, jisne fatah ki thi who manzile

11. ज़िंदगी का सफर

ऐसे ज़िंदगी चल पड़ी
एक पल न मिला, कुछ समझ पाऊँ
कोसूँ यह कराहू
किस पर उंगली उठाऊँ

वो सपने जो दम तोड़ गए
यह अपने जो मुँह मोड़ गए
रूठूँ तो किससे
ख़ुद से या क़िस्मत से

ना सोचा था यह होगी मेरी राहें
कब जाने चुन ली मैंने आहें
हार है यह है यही रीत
छूट गया कहीं, जो चाहा था संगीत

लगा था कि बदल दूँगी दुनिया
तब थी एक छोटी सी मुन्निया
अब है रूठी सी यह ज़िंदगी
कैसे बनाऊ अब इससे हँसी?

12. Zindagi Ka Safar

Aise zindagi chal padi
Ek pal na mila kuch samajh pau
Kosu yeah karahu
Kis par ungli uthauu

Woh sapne jo dam tod gaye
Yeah apne jo muh mod gaye
Ruthu toh kissse
Khud se yeah kismat se

Na soocha tha yeah hogi meri rahe
Kab jane chunlee maine aahe
Haar hai yeah hai yehi reet
Chut gaya kahi, jo chaha tha sangeet

Laga tha ki badal dungi duniya
Tab thi ek choti se muniya
Ab hai ruthi si yeah zindagi
Kaise banau ab isse hassi?

13. अलविदा

कह पाती एक बार अलविदा
दो पल मिल जाते जो, होने से पहले जुदा
मरहम सा मिल जाता,
जीने के लिए

इस दिलासे में है कि तुम्हारा साया था
तुमने उंगली थामी थी मेरी, इंसान बनाया था
कैसे जिएँगे तुम्हारे बिना
ये तुमने सिखाया कहाँ

कह पाती एक बार अलविदा
दो पल मिल जाते जो, होने से पहले जुदा
ढूँढ लेती उन लम्हों में कोई सहारा
टीस न होती कम, दर्द होता दोबारा

आँसू जो दिखते हैं आँखों में मेरे
कैसे रोकूँ, ये तो मेरे सीने से बहें
दस्तक कोई होती है सोचती हूँ तुम हो
आँचल तुम्हारा कहीं लहराता सा लगे

तुम्हारी याद भी एक तोहफ़ा
कैसे इन्हें समेटूँ, बाँहों में भरु
जो दिल में लाए दर्द का है तुफ़ा
लगता है जैसे चीख़ता है आसमान

जब तक साँस है, तुम्हारा एहसास है
तुम चले गए, पर आज भी वो लम्हे ख़ास हैं
पर कह पाती एक बार अलविदा
दो पल मिल जाते जो, होने से पहले जुदा

14. Alvida

Keh paati ek baar alvida
Do pal mil jate jo, ho ne se pehle juda
Murhum sa mil jata,
Jeene ke liye

Is dilase mein hai ki tumhara saya tha
Tum ne ungli thami thi meri, insaan banya tha
Kaise jeyenge tumhare bina
Yeh tumne sikhaya kaha

Keh paati ek baar alvida
Do pal mil jate jo, ho ne se pehle juda
Dhunde leti un lamho mein koi sahara
Tees na hoti kam, dard hota dubara

Aasu jo dikhte hai aanhko mein mere
Kaise roku yeh toh mere seene se bahe
Dastak koi hoti hai sochati hu tum ho
Aanchal tumhare kahi lehrata sa lage

Tumhari yaad bhi ek tofah
Kaise inhe samatu, baho mein bharu
Jo dil mein laye dard ka hai tufah
Lagta hai jaise cheekhta hai aasman

Jab tak saans hai, tumhara ehsaas hai
Tum chale gaye, pur aaj bhi woh lamhe kaas hai
Pur keh paati ek baar alvida
Do pal mil jate jo, ho ne se pehle juda

15. शाम, रात और सुबह

आज फिर शाम उदास है
बिखरे हुए कुछ जज़्बात हैं
रौशनी के जाने का
दर्द भी सीने के पास है

डर है कहीं ये आनेवाला अंधकार ही जीवन न बन जाए
कैसे मैं इस रौशनी को फिर लाऊँ
क्यों है ये तन्हाई, जो साँसों को है घेरे
लगता है जैसे, आँसू सूख गए हैं मेरे

आज फिर शाम उदास है
बिखरे हुए कुछ जज़्बात हैं
मन में उठे कई सवाल हैं
क्या ये रात छोड़ेगी, या तोड़ेगी मुझे

अंधेरा है जैसे बढ़ता
म्यूसियत भी है जकड़ती
लगता है वक़्त रुक ही गया है
तभी बजी बारह बजे की घंटी

आधी रात हो गई
उदासी में, सवालों को टटोलते वक़्त आगे बढ़ गया
ख़याल ये आया, कुछ ही रात बाक़ी है
फिर तो सूरज आएगा

आज फिर शाम उदास थी
बिखरे हुए कुछ जज़्बात थे
पर कभी तो रौशनी आएगी
दर्द को भी सीने से ले जाएगी

16. Shaam, Raat Aur Subah

Aaj phir shaam udas hai
Bikhare hue kuch jazbaat hai
Roshini ke jaane ka
Dard bhi seene ke pass hai

Darr hai kahi yeh aanewala andhkar, hee jeevan na ban jaye
Kaise mein iss roshini ko phir lau
Kyu hai yeh tanhai, jo sasoo ko hai ghere
Lagta hai jaise, aasu sukh gaye hai mere

Aaj phir shaam udas hai
Bikhare hue kuch jazbaat hai
Mann mein uthe kai sawaal hai
Kya yeah raat chode gee, yeah todegee mujhe

Andhera hai jaise badhta
Mayusiyat bhi hai jakarti
Lagta hai waqt ruk hi gaya hai
Tabhi baji barah baje ki ghanti

Aadhi raat ho gayi
Udassi mein, sawalo ko tatolte waqt aage badh gaya
Khayal yeah aaya, kuch hi raat baki hai

Phir toh suraj aayega

Aaj phir shaam udas thi
Bekhare hue kuch jazbaat thee
Pur kabhi toh roshini aayegi
Dard ko bhi seene se le ja

17. खामोश रिश्ता

कुछ रिश्ता था हमारा दूर का
टूटा नहीं, न बिखरा ही
पर जुदा से रहे हमेशा

कभी प्यार सा, कभी मलाल सा
कभी दर्द दिया, कभी भुला दिया

वो धागा भी आज टूट गया
पर ग़म ने मुझे नहीं छुआ
ना ही रही दिल में कोई शिकायत
कई बार सोचा
क्यों खालीपन ने हमें छोड़ दिया

जीते रहे हम दो किनारों पे
जो जिया ही नहीं
उसे हम भुला सकते क्या कभी?

18. Khamosh Rishta

Kuch rishta tha hamara dur ka
Tuta nahi, na bikhra hi
Par juda se rahe hamesha

Kabhi pyaar sa kabhi malal sa
Kabhi dard diya, kabhi bhula diya

Woh dhaga bhi Aaj Tut gaya
Par gum ne mujhe nahi chua
Na hi rahi Dil mein koi shikayat

Kai baar socha
kyu khalipan ne hame chod diya

Jeete rahe hum do kinaro pe
Jo jiya hi nahi
Usse hum bhula sakte kya kabhi

19. एक नई शुरुआत

कर रही एक नई शुरुआत
उम्मीद है पर डर भी है साथ
कोशिश का दामन हूँ थामे
पहला क़दम बढ़ाऊँ

लगता है जैसे मंज़िल है बुलाए
पर कुछ बढ़ते ही, हम हैं लड़खड़ाए
कैसे सोच लिया हमने, कि ये कर पाए
मायूस मन ने तो रोक दिया

कोई कह गया, अभी तो शुरुआत है
कोशिश करो, उसी में बात है
एक और क़दम बढ़ाया
फिर लगा मंज़िल ने बुलाया

बात आई समझ में,
कभी लड़खड़ाऊँ, कभी अव्वल हो जाऊँ
कोशिश की राह है,
अभी तो शुरुआत है

20. Ek Nayi Shuruwat

Kar Rahi ek nai shuruwat
Umeed hai par dar bhi hai saath
Koshish ka daman hu thame
Pehla kadam badhau

Lagta hai jaise manzil hai bulae
Par kuch badte hi, hum hai ladkhadae
Kaise soch liya hum ne, ki yeh kar paye
Mayus mann ne toh rook diya

Koi keh gaya, abhi toh shuruwat hai
Koshish karo, usi mein baat hai
Ek aur kadam badhaya
Phir laga manzil ne bulaya

Baat aaee samajh mein,
Kabhi ladkhadu, kabhi awal ho jau
Koshish ki raah hai,
Abhi toh shuruwat hai

21. अभी तो मंज़िले बाकी हैं

अभी तो मंज़िले बाकी हैं
नहीं है थकने की आज़ादी
बढ़ना है आगे
भले धीमी हो चाल

रुकना है नहीं
चाहे लगे रहे विशाल
सही दिशा में राह है लेनी
बस है चलते रहना

डरने की ना है ज़रूरत
रोज़ करनी है कोशिश
फिर कैसे ना मिलेंगी चाहत
सिर उठाए बढ़ेंगे फ़ौलादी

करनी है मेहनत
जैसे हो पूजा
मिलेंगे तुमको
सारी दुनिया ही

लक्ष्य पे रखे नजर
जीत होगी तेरे द्वार
रहो तुम तत्पर
केंद्रित रहो है पल

अभी तो मंज़िले बाकी हैं
नहीं है थकने की आज़ादी
बढ़ना है आगे
भले धीमी हो चाल

22. Abhi Toh Manzile Baki Hai

Abhi toh manzile baki hai
Nahi hai thakne ki azadi
Badhna hai aage
Bhale dhimi ho chal

Rukna hai nahi
Chahe lage rahe vishal
Sahi disha mein raah hai leni
Bus hai chalte rahna

Darne ki na hai zaroorat
Roz karni hai koshish
Phir kaise na milengi chahat
Sir uthae badhenge fauladi

Karni hai mehnat
Jaise ho pooja
Milge tumko
Saari duniya hee

Lakshya pe rakhe nazar
Jeet hogi tere dar par
Raho tum tatpar

Kendrit raho hai pal

Abhi toh manzile baki hai
Nahi hai thakne ki azadi
Badhna hai aage
Bhale dhimi ho chal

23. कोशिश ही जीत

दर्पण ने फिर याद दिलाया
बनानी मुझे अपनी तक़दीर है
जीतना तो मुश्किल है
पर हारकर जीना क्या ज़िंदगी कहलाएगा?

एक बार छुई थी जो ऊँचाइयाँ
उन्हें फिर पाने की हिम्मत भी नहीं है
पर कब तक बीते वक़्त के सहारे चलते जाऊँ
फिर एक और कोशिश करूँ
भले हार जाऊँ

पर फिर हार ही बन जाएगी ये ज़िंदगी
ये बीते लम्हों को निहारूँ और उसी को मानूँ
जो चला गया, वही था मेरा सफ़र
कब तक ख़ुद को ये छलावा दिखाऊँ?

हिम्मत जुटाकर, फिर आज हारने के लिए तैयार हो जाऊँ
शायद किस्मत न खिले
पर ये सुकून तो मिले, कि आगे बढ़ने की कोशिश से न डर जाऊँ

24. Koshish Hee Jeet

Darpan ne fir yaad dilaya
Banani mujhe apni takdir hai
Jeetna toh mushkil hai
Pur haarkar jeena, kya zindagi kehlaye ga

Ek baar chuei thi jo ucchaiya
Unhe fir pane ki himmat bhi nahi hai
Par kab tak beete waqt ke sahere chalte jau
Phir ek aur koshish karu
Bhale haar jau

Par phir haar hee, ban jayega yeh zindagi
Yeah beete lamhe ko niharu, aur usi ko maanu
Jo chala gaya wahi tha mere safar
Kab tak khud ko yeh chalawa dikhau?

Himmat juta kar, phir aaj harne ke liye tyaar ho jau
Shayad kismat na khile
Pur yeah sukun toh mile, ki aage badhne ki koshish se na dar jau

25. सूरज की सवारी

वक्त जब है बदलता
सूरज सा अकेला ही है तू ढलता
आसमान में ली थी जो उड़ान
उसका तो कर सकोगे बखान

पर शाम की एक चादर ओढ़े
उठेगा मन में तूफ़ान
कभी बहेंगी आँखों से कुछ बूँदें
जब बीती बुलंदियों के सामने हो जाओगे बेज़ुबान

अब तो तुम उतर चुके हो ढलान
रास्ता फिर भी दे सकता है एक अरमान
ढूँढो फिर से उस रोशनी को
हो सकता है कोई किरण दे जाए नया फ़रमान

लेकर एक इरादा, खुद से करो एक वादा
कोशिश करो पूरी, हो सकता है, ना हो अब दूरी
जैसे तुम क़दम बढ़ाओ, और कभी लड़खड़ाओ
मान लो ये बात, जीवन भी देती है साथ

मदद का हाथ बढ़िए
प्रेरणा कोई मिल जाए
फिर से नए वक्त में करना
सूरज की सवारी

26. Suraj Ki Sawari

Waqt jab hai badalta
Suraj sa akela hi hai tu dhalta
Asmaan mein lee thi jo udaan
Uska toh kar sakoge bakhan

Par shaam ki ek chadar odhe
Udhega mann mein tufan
Kabhi bahengi aanko se kuch bunde
Jab biti bulandio ke samne ho jaoge bezuban

Ab toh tum utar chuke ho dhalan
Rasta phir bhi de sakta hai ek armaan
Dundo phir se uss roshani ko
Ho sakta hai koi kiran de jaye naya pharmaan

Lekar ek irrada, khud se karo ek wada
Koshish karo puri, ho sakta hai na ho ab duri
Jaise tum kadam badhao, aur kabhi ladkhadao
Maan lo yeh baat, jeevan bhi deti hai saath

Maddat ka hath badhaye
Prerna koi mil jaye
Phir se naye waqt mein karna
Suraj ki sawari

27. सच्ची इबादत

करते हैं इबादत
ख़ुदा के नाम की
दो लफ़्ज़ हमदर्दी के
बोलो उसके बंदों के साथ भी

खूबसूरत वही है इंसान
दुनिया के सामने ही नहीं
सबको बराबर देता है इज़्ज़त
चाहे कमजोर हो कोई

उसके दर पे जाकर सुकून मांगते हैं
पर दूसरों का चैन छीनते, घबराते नहीं
कैसे सुनेगा वो इबादत
जब तक एक सच्चा इंसान की आवाज़ न हो

वो देख रहा है, हर पल
अब बदल जाओ, नेकी पे चलो
करो सच्ची इबादत
अपने दिल में भी राहत पाओ

करते हैं इबादत
ख़ुदा के नाम की
पर रुक जाते हैं कुछ लफ़्ज़ बोल कर
क्यूँ नहीं दिखती ये रहमदिली

उसके बंदों के और भी?

जो आँसू दे जाए दूसरों को
उनको कैसे मिले सुकून

करते हैं इबादत
ख़ुदा के नाम की
दो लफ़्ज़ इंसानियत के
कर देंगे जिंदगी को बेहतरीन

28. Sacchi Ibadat

Karte hain ibadat
Khuda ke naam ki
Do lafz humdardi ke
Bolo uske bando ke saath bhi

Khubsoorat wohi hai insaan
Duniya ke saamne hi nahi
Sabko barabar deta ho izzat
Chahe kamzor ho koi

Uske dar pe jaake sukoon maangte hain
Par doosron ka chain cheente, ghabrate nahi
Kaise sunega woh ibadat
Jab tak ek saccha insaan ki aawaaz na ho

Woh dekh raha hai, har pal
Ab badal jao, neeki pe chalo
Karo sacchi ibadat
Apne dil mein bhi rahat pao

Karte hain ibadat
Khuda ke naam ki
Par ruk jaate hain kuch lafz bol kar
Kyu nahi dikhti yeh rehamdili

Uske bando ke aur bhi?

Jo aansu de jaaye doosron ko
Unko kaise mile sukoon

Karte hain ibadat
Khuda ke naam ki
Do lafz insaniyat ke
Kar denge zindagi ko behtereein

29. छोटी सी उंगलियों

उन छोटी उंगलियों से जब तूने थामा मेरा हाथ
सहारा मिल गया मुझे
जुड़ गई किस्मत तेरे साथ

ग़मों को फेंक दिया तूने दूर
राहों में भर दिए फूल
ताक़त एक ऐसी आ गई
हिम्मत करने की नीयत भा गई

तेरी छोटी हँसी ने
संगीत भर दिया घर में
डर को कर दिया दूर
दे दी ख़ुशी, छा गया एक सुरूर

बना दिया मुझे ख़ुशहाल
बन गई तू मेरी ढाल
ताक़त बन गई मेरी लड़ने की
गिर के फिर उभरने की

जब से आए हो मेरी गोद में
जीने का मक़सद मिल गया मुझे
उन छोटी उंगलियों से जब तूने थामा मेरा हाथ
साथ तेरा बेहतर बना गया मुझे

30. Choti See Ungulio

Un choti ungulio se, jab tune thama mere hath
Sahara mil gaya mujhe
Jud gai kismat tere saath

Gamo ko phek diya tune dur
Raho mein bhar diye phool
Taakat ek aisi aagi
Himmat karne neeyat bhaa gayi

Tere choti hasi ne
Sangeet bhar diya ghar mein
Darr ko kar diya dur
Dedi khushi, chaya ek suruur

Bana diya mujhe khushaaal
Ban gayi tu meri dhal
Taakat ban gayi meri ladne ki
Girke phir ubharne ki

Jab se aaye ho meri good mein
Jeene ka maksad mil gaya mujhe
Un choti ungulio se jab, tune thama mere hath
Sath tera behtar bana gaya mujhe

31. दोस्ती का सुकून

दोस्त न होते तो क्या होती ये दुनिया
किसे सुनते हम अपनी हर फ़िक्र
कौन मानता हमारे बेतुकी बातों को
कैसे करते हम ख़ामोशी में ज़िक्र

सूना सा होता ये जहाँ
हँसी छुप जाती कहीं
दिल में ही रह जाते दर्द बेपनाह
खो जाते हम भी यहीं

जीते हम बिल्कुल तन्हा
कैसे मिलता ये सुकून,
कि किसी को है हमारी फ़िक्र

कौन देता हमें हौसला
कौन दिखाता हमारी ग़लतियाँ
कोई तो जो सुनता है हमें

दोस्त न होते तो क्या होती ये दुनिया
किसे सुनते हम अपनी हर फ़िक्र
कौन मानता हमारे बेतुकी बातों को
कैसे करते हम ख़ामोशी में ज़िक्र

32. Dosti Ka Sukoon

Dost na hote toh kya hoti yeh duniya
Kise sunte hum apni har fikar
Kaun manta hamari betuki bato ko
Kaise karte hum khomoshi mein zikre

Suna sa hota yeah jaha
Hasi chup jati kahi
Dil mein hee reh jate dard bepanha
Kho jate hum bhi yahi

Jeete hum bulkul tanha
Kaise milta yeah sukun,
ki kissi ko hai hamari fikar
Kaun deta hame hosla
Kaun dikhata hamari galtiya
Koi toh jo sunta hai hame

Dost na hote toh kya hoti yeh duniya
Kise sunte hum apni har fikar
Kaun Manta hamare betuki bato ko
Kaise karte hum khomoshi mein zikre

33. साथी तुम, सहारा तुम

तुम ही थे, ना जब था कोई साथ
तुम ही थे, जब ना थामा किसी ने मेरा हाथ
जब मैं टूटी, जब मैं रोई
तुम ही थे जिसने जोड़े टुकड़े मेरे हर रात

हर दर्द में, हर डर में
समझाई मुझे हर बात
मंज़िल ही नहीं, राह भी तुम
हर उम्मीद, हर रौशनी का एहसास भी तुम

तुम ही थे, ना जब था कोई साथ
तुम ही थे, जब ना थामा किसी ने मेरा हाथ
जब मैं टूटी, जब मैं रोई
तुम ही थे जिसने जोड़े टुकड़े मेरे हर रात

मन मेरे तुम ही थे मेरे साथी
जब मैं रोए, खुद ही पोछे मैंने आँसू
मन मेरे तुम ही थे सहारा
जब कोई और न था हमारा

34. Sathi Tum, Sahara Tum

Tum hee the, na jab tha koi saath
Tum hee the, jab na thama kisi ne mera haath
Jab main tuti, jab main roi
Tum hee the, jisne jode tukre mere har raat

Har dard mein har darr mein
Samjhai mujhe har baat
Manzil hee nahi, raah bhi tum
Har Umeed, har roshni ka ehsaas bhi tum

Tum hee the, na jab tha koi saath
Tum hee the, jab na thama kisi ne mera haath
Jab main tuti, jab main roi
Tum hee the, jisne jode tukre mere har raat

Mann mere tum hi the mere saathi
Jab main roee, khud hi poche maine aasu
Mann mere tum hi the sahara
Jab koi aur na tha hamara

35. आसमान की पहचान

उड़ते हुए परिंदे ने पूछा आसमान से
क्यों नहीं छू पाता मैंने तेरी ऊँचाई
कितना भी पंख फड़फड़ाऊँ, पर तुझे दूर ही पाऊँ

आसमान बोला – ये दूरी ही मेरी पहचान है
मैं विशाल हूँ, बिखरा हुआ
सबका आसमान, पर कोई मेरा नहीं

दूर हूँ, क्यूंकि दुनिया बस मुझे देखना चाहती है
ऊँचा हूँ, कि इंसान की प्रेरणा बनूँ
मैं अमर हूँ, हर पल रहूँ

तुम इंसान की तरह जीवित हो
जीने की, मरने की, हारने की, डरने की
सबकी आज़ादी है तुम्हें

मैं सदा वही हूँ
दूरी ही मेरी पहचान है
मैं विशाल हूँ, बिखरा हुआ
मैं सबका आसमान हूँ

36. Aasmaan Ki Pehchaan

Udte hue parinde ne pucha aasmaan se
Kyu nahin chu paata maine teri uchahi
Kitna bhi pankh farfadu, par tujhe duur hi pau

Aasmaan bola, yeh duri hee meri pehchan hai
Mein vishal hu, bikhra hua
Sabka aasmaan pur, koi mera nahi

Dur hu, kunki duniya bas mujhe dekhna chahti hai
Uccha hu, ki insaan ki prerna banu
Main amar hu, har pal rahu

Tum insaan ki tarah jeevit ho
Jeene ki, marne ki, haarne ki, darne ki
Sab ki, aazadi hai tumhe

Main sada wahi hu
Duri hee meri pehchan hai
Mein vishal hu, bikhra hua
Main sabka aasmaan hu

37. शायर का हुनर

शायर हूँ, कोई ग़ज़ल लिखवा लो
दिल चाहे तो कोई दोहा बढ़वा लो
चादर, तौलिये और रुमाल धुलवाओगे
या हमसे रोटियाँ सिकवाओगे?

कैसे तुम्हें सुनाऊँ अफ़साना
तुमने बर्तन सफ़ाई के अलावा मुझे नहीं जाना
कभी तो हमारे हुनर का काम करवा लो
ना करो उम्मीद कि सफ़ाई कर दें

पहचानों हमें,
झाड़ू की नहीं, क़लम की आदत है हमें
लिख सकते हैं कुछ ऐसा, जो दिल बहला दे
तुम्हारे होठों पे मुस्कान ला दे

जब थके आओ शाम को
तुम्हारे लिए कुछ नग़मे गुनगुना दूँ
पर तुम आते ही कह गए – चाय बना दे!

38. Shayar Ka Hunar

Shayar hu, koi ghazal likh wa lo
Dil chahe toh koi doha badhwalo
Chadar, taulie aur rumal dhulwo ge
Yeah hum se rotiya sikwao ge

Kaise tumhe sunau afsana
Tumne bartan-safai ke alawa mujhe nahi jana
Kabhi toh hamare hunar ka kaam karwa lo
Na karo umeed ki safai kar de

Pehchano hame,
Jhadu ki nahi, kalam ki aadat hai hame
Likh sakte hai kuch aisa, Jo dil behla de
Tumhare hothon pe muskan la de

Jab thake auo saham ko
Tumhare liye kuch nagme gunguna du
Par tum aate hee keh gaye, chai bana de!

39. सावन

सूखी सी ये पत्तियाँ
कर रही तेरे इंतज़ार
रिमझिम तू बरसे
सावन में मेघ मल्हार

तपती धूप है, सूरज दिखा रहा अपनी ताक़त
सूखा है, हारा सा, हर नज़ारा
प्यास है बन गई साथी

अब थका गई है ये गर्मी
मिले इन साँसों को राहत
आजा अब ओ सावन
बरसों ऐसे कि शीतल कर दो ज़मीन को

मेरे बुलाने का कुछ तो दो जवाब
कर रही हूँ धरती संग, मैं भी तेरा इंतज़ार

क्या सुना ये मैंने?
धीमी सी एक आहट हुई

कैसी ये सरसराहट हुई
हवा क्यों है मचली सी
क्या बूंदों की दस्तक हुई?

सोंधी एक महक, सुकून तो दे गई
बारिश आई, ज़मीन को भिगो गई
सुकून भी मिला कुछ पल का

ऐसा ही सावन आए ज़िंदगी में
करे चिंताओं को दूर, करे मन को शांत
सूखी जीवन की पत्तियाँ को में ले आए रंग

40. Sawan

Sukhi see yeah patiya
Kar rahi tere intezaar
Rim jhim tu barse
Sawan mein megh malhaar

Tapti dhoop hai, suraj dikha raha apni taakat
Sukha hai, haara sa her nazara
Pyass hai ban gayi saathi

Ab thaka gayi hai yeah garmi
Mille in saaso ko rahat
Aaja ab o sawan
Barso aise ki sheetal kar do zameen ko

Mere bulane ka kuch toh do jawaab
Kar rahi hu dharti sung, main bhi tera intezaar
Kya suna yeh maine?

Dheemi si ek aahat Hui
Kaisi yeh sarsarahat Hui
Hawa kyu hai machali si
Kya bundo ki dastak hui?

Sondhi ek mehak, sukoon toh de gayi

Baarish aayi zameen ko bhigo gayi
Sukoon bhi mila kuch pal ka

Aisa hee sawan aaye zindagi mein
Kare chintao ko dur, kare mann ko shant
Sukhi jeevan ki patiya ko mein le aaye rang

41. पुकार

रोशन सी ये राहें
किसको है पुकारे
आसमान भी है जैसे
खिलखिलाता, बाँहे फैलाए

सूरज उगने से पहले
करता है किसका इंतज़ार
ये पहाड़ भी, बैठे किससे आस लगाए

झरने बहते-बहते
करते किस की बातें
कहीं तो छुपा हुआ है
जिसको सब बुलाते

कभी ये तुमने जाना
तेरे लिए ही है ये क़ायनात
तेरी ही आगे बढ़ने का
वक़्त भी करता है इंतज़ारये बात तू जान ले
आगे क़दम बढ़ा ले
तेरे लिए ही है ये जहाँ
बाँहें फैलाए खड़ा, आसमान

ख़ुद को तू पहचान
तेरे लिए ही रोशन राहें

ना समझ ख़ुद को हारा, थका, लाचार
सूरज कहता है तुझे पुकार

जाग ओ इंसान, ताक़त अपनी समेट
कर ख़ुद पे भरोसा
बोल रहे हैं झरने
तेरे लिए ही रोशन हैं राहें
तुझे ऐ उम्मीद करता है ब्रह्मांड

अब तू भी बढ़
बना अपनी पहचान!

42. Pukar

Roshan see yeh rahe
Kisko hai pukare
Aasman bhi hai jaise
Khilkhilata bahe phailaye

Suraj ugne se pehle
Karta hai kiska intezaar
Yeh pahad bhi, baithe kiss se aas lagaye

Jharne behte behte
Karte kiss ki baate
Kahi toh chupa hua hai
Jisko sab bulate

Kabhi yeh tum ne jana
Tere liye hee hai yeh kainaat
Teri hee aage badhne ka
Waqt bhi karta hai intezaar

Yeh baat tu jaan lee
Aage kadam badha lee
Tere liye hee hai yeh jahan
Bahe phailaye khada aasmaan

Khud ko tu pehchan
Tere liye hi roshan rahe
Na samjhe khud ko hara, thaka, lacchar
Suraj kehta hai tujhe pukar

Jag o insaan, taakat apni samet,
Kar khud pe bharosa,
Bol rahe hai jharne

Tere liye hee roshan hai rahe
Tuje hee se umeed karta hai bramhand

Ab tu bhi badh,
Bana apni pehchan!

www.ingramcontent.com/pod-product-compliance
Lightning Source LLC
Chambersburg PA
CBHW070645240926
51846CB00003BA/795
9789371563758